PRAYING WITH THE CHURCH
THROUGH ADVENT

D1602535

Fr. Edward Looney

PRAYING

WITH THE

CHURCH

THROUGH

ADVENT

SOPHIA INSTITUTE PRESS
Manchester, New Hampshire

Sophia Institute Press

Box 5284, Manchester, NH 03108

1-800-888-9344

www.SophiaInstitute.com

Sophia Institute Press is a registered trademark of Sophia Institute.

paperback ISBN 979-8-88911-324-9

ebook ISBN 979-8-88911-325-6

Library of Congress Control Number: 2024942543

First printing

CONTENTS

Propers of Saints

PRAYING WITH THE CHURCH
THROUGH ADVENT

INTRODUCTION

atholics have been preparing for special liturgical feast days for centuries. Two principal feast days have built-in seasons to help us prepare for them: Advent, which precedes Christmas, and Lent, which precedes Easter. When an individual wishes to consecrate his life to Jesus through Mary by any consecration methods available (St. Louis de Montfort, St. Maximilian Kolbe, Fr. Gaitley, etc.), they choose a Marian date, and for thirty-three days, they pray and prepare. Sometimes they celebrate the feast days of saints on the calendar by praying a novena, a prayer or cycle of prayers that is repeated over nine days before the feast day and that asks the saint for a special grace. When it comes to Christmas, not only do we have Advent, but also the St. Andrew's Novena prayer that begins on November 30 and is prayed until Christmas.

There are numerous Advent devotionals that have been published over the years. My favorite is titled *Come, Lord Jesus: Meditations on the Art of Waiting* by Mother Mary Francis. If

you want to learn more about her, I'd encourage you to check out my book *How They Love Mary: 28 Life-Changing Stories of Devotion to Our Lady* in which I provide her Marian profile. I also enjoyed *Advent with Our Lady of Fatima* by Donna-Marie Cooper O'Boyle, which inspired my Lenten book, *A Lenten Journey with Mother Mary*. For years, Catholic parishes in the United States have provided little blue books for Advent and black books for Lent, originally published by the Diocese of Saginaw by Bishop Ken Untener. As a pastor, I have seen any good number of Advent resources. Yet, here I am, offering another contribution to the genre of devotional literature.

When we gather for Mass, after the penitential rite or the Gloria, that is, the final part of the introductory rites, the priest says or chants, "Let us pray." We often refer to this as the opening prayer, but it is officially called the Collect. As an entire congregation has gathered in prayer, the priest collects the prayers and summarizes them in this prayer to God. These Collects are written for each Sunday in Ordinary Time and typically a saint will have a special one for his memorial or feast. If you know something about the saint, you often can find biographical hints in them. For example, for the memorial of St. John Neumann, who served as bishop of Philadelphia, the phrase "brotherly love" is in the prayer. The Collect for St. John of the Cross refers to one of his spiritual writings.

What is unique about the seasons of Advent and Lent, Christmas and Easter, is that the Church offers a special Collect, prayer over the gifts, prayer after Communion, and prayer over the people. Every day the prayer is different. I have preached on the prayers and reflected on them at times. This book is a collection of those Collects from the Mass, and I offer a reflection on one aspect of the prayer and provide a few reflection questions for you to consider, perhaps using a prayer journal.

My aim in writing this Advent meditation book is to make these reflections accessible. A meditation that would be a few pages might be too time-consuming for an individual. My hope is that you make a cup of coffee, sit down with this book, pray the Collect, reflect on the words, and spend a few moments in quiet prayer mulling over the question. If it doesn't happen over coffee, this would be a good companion for daily Mass. Arrive at Mass a little early. If the Rosary is prayed beforehand, hopefully there is enough time for your quiet prayer and reflection before Mass begins. You can then pray over the Collect that will be prayed at that Mass (unless it's a required memorial). Or if you want to

allow the fruits of Mass to linger a bit longer, you can remain in your pew after Mass for a few moments of prayer and reflection, revisiting the Collect prayer.

I have chosen to omit most celebrations of the saints, even if they are required memorials (e.g., St. Ambrose). The proper of saints that I have included in this manuscript includes the two Marian feasts of the Immaculate Conception and Our Lady of Guadalupe. These can be found at the end of the main text, beginning on page 183.

My hope as you make your way through this Advent devotional is that you will better appreciate the texts of the Mass and that on any Sunday or daily Mass that you might attend throughout the year, you will listen more attentively to the opening prayer and reflect upon it yourself. And if you enjoyed this Advent devotional, be sure to look for the sister book for Lent, where I do the same thing: present the Collect, reflect, and encourage meditation. May your Advent be blessed and as the Church prays on December 24, "May the Lord come quickly and not delay!"

FIRST SUNDAY
OF ADVENT

TODAY'S COLLECT

Grant your faithful, we pray, almighty God,
the resolve to run forth to meet your Christ
with righteous deeds at his coming,
so that, gathered at his right hand,
they may be worthy to possess the heavenly kingdom.

oday begins the season of Advent. In a secular sense, the world has already been preparing for Christmas by listening to Christmas music or getting prepared for upcoming celebrations. Our observance of religious Advent allows us to prepare our hearts spiritually through prayer, devotion, and celebration of the sacraments. A lot of Catholics will choose to celebrate the Sacrament of Reconciliation before Christmas, detaching themselves from sin and the past.

Another way people will prepare for Christmas is through generosity and helping others. In this season of the year, people wish to give more. We don't want to be like the old Ebenezer Scrooge who didn't want to help anyone, but we want to be the transformed Scrooge who is generous to all. We see it especially with giving trees, which contain tags of items that individuals who have fallen on hard times would like to receive. For those moms and dads who are unable to buy gifts for their children, the aid of people who have a little extra to give helps them not to dwell on their

current situation and will put a happy face on their children on Christmas morning.

What we pray for on this first Sunday of Advent is that we will be ready to run forth to meet Christ with righteous deeds at His coming. Generosity toward others is just one of these righteous deeds that we can present to the Lord. The teaching of Jesus in Matthew 25 reminds us that when we feed the hungry or clothe the naked, we did it for Jesus. If you are able, help someone this Christmas, and in so doing, you will be helping Christ, who has come to you in that moment, and whose return we still await.

Reflection Questions

1. Do you know someone personally who has fallen on hard times? Is there anything you can do to help them? Would they openly accept your help or would it have to be subtle and anonymous?

   _____

   _____

   _____

   _____

2. Does your Church or an area business offer a giving tree that you could participate in to help a local impoverished family?

   _____

   _____

   _____

   _____

3. What other righteous deeds could you do this Advent besides charitable giving?

_____

_____

_____

_____

MONDAY OF THE FIRST WEEK OF ADVENT

Keep us alert, we pray, O Lord our God,
as we await the advent of Christ your Son,
so that, when he comes and knocks,
he may find us watchful in prayer
and exultant in his praise.

popular devotional image of Jesus has Him knocking on the door of someone's home. A close inspection of the picture by the viewer will see that there is no doorknob on the exterior, it's only on the interior. This image could be a depiction of Revelation 3:20, where it says, "Behold, I stand at the door and knock; if any one hears my voice and opens the door, I will come in to him and eat with him, and he with me." Jesus wants to come in. He could force His way in. But instead, He wants to ask your permission. He gently knocks at the door, hoping that you will let Him in. He has a lot to say and do with you. But you have to be ready for Him to say and do these things. Often, we might feel the gentle nudge of God in our life. It could be around a particular sin, and the nudge is Jesus moving us toward conversion. It's His knock, on your heart, on your soul, and if you wish you can open the door.

During this Advent season, Jesus might want to come and knock on the door of your heart and soul. Today's

Collect draws our attention to the nature of Christ's eventual return in glory at the end of time. We want to stay alert so that we are not caught off guard when Christ comes and knocks at the end of time. I am willing to bet that you have had that awkward experience when someone knocks on your door and as you go to answer, you pass by an unkept living room— maybe you have laundry on the couch that is in the process of being folded, or you haven't cleaned up from making lunch or dinner in the kitchen. You don't know who the visitor knocking is, and you get a little embarrassed about opening the door. We don't want that to happen when Jesus comes. Be alert. You can do this by thinking, Jesus might be coming. Am I ready for Him? When He knocks, may He find you watchful in prayer. How are you praying? Is your spiritual house ready for a visit from Jesus?

Reflection Questions

1. Do you have a prayer corner in your home? Is this something that would be useful to you and help you cultivate a spirit of being watchful in prayer?

   _____

   _____

   _____

   _____

2. In what ways have you prayed in your home this past week? Perhaps keep a journal to log how you are keeping watch in prayer.

   _____

   _____

   _____

   _____

3. What spiritual cleaning do you need to do to have your
   spiritual house prepared for Jesus to visit?

   _____

   _____

   _____

   _____

TUESDAY OF THE
FIRST WEEK OF ADVENT

Look with favor, Lord God, on our petitions,
and in our trials grant us your compassionate help,
that, consoled by the presence of your Son,
whose coming we now await,
we may be tainted no longer
by the corruption of former ways.

The Letter to the Hebrews tells us that we have a high priest who can sympathize with our weaknesses, one who was tried in every way but did not sin (Heb. 4:15). This is the gift of the Incarnation. Jesus, the second Person of the Trinity, the Son of God, came to earth and lived our life. Consequently, He knows the struggles of our human existence.

In Christology, there is a special term called the *soteriological principle*, which teaches that what is not assumed is not redeemed. Essentially, what this means is that when Jesus entered the human condition, He assumed it all in His Divine Person so that it could be redeemed. He assumed sadness, so that it could be redeemed. He assumed grieving, so that it could be redeemed. Jesus underwent His own set of trials. He experienced the death of St. Joseph and St. John the Baptist. He learned about Lazarus's passing away and wept. He was betrayed by a friend and handed over to be

killed. All of this, having been assumed by Jesus, now has been redeemed by Him.

During these Advent days, you may be praying to the Lord with specific petitions during your own trial that you are facing. Look to Jesus, His life, His story, and His example. From Him, draw your strength. In Him, in the Eucharist, find your support. Allow the Lord to console you with His compassionate help, help that comes from Him because He already suffered it, but also because now He suffers with you in this trial. Spend a few minutes thinking of and talking to the Lord Jesus about your trial with the hope that He will not abandon you and will come to your aid.

Reflection Questions

1. What message is Jesus giving you during the trial that you are facing? How is He giving you hope?

_____

_____

_____

_____

2. What has tainted you as an individual? What has corrupted you?

_____

_____

_____

_____

3. How can you move on from your former ways into the freedom that Christ is calling you to right now?

_____

_____

_____

_____

WEDNESDAY OF THE FIRST WEEK OF ADVENT

Today's Collect

Prepare our hearts, we pray, O Lord our God,
by your divine power,
so that at the coming of Christ your Son
we may be found worthy of the banquet of eternal life
and merit to receive heavenly nourishment from his hands.

$\mathfrak{C}$lose your eyes for a moment and think about this question: What do you picture Heaven to be like? We have all been to the funeral where a speaker suggests that Heaven will be fishing on a big lake or endless rounds of golf. I'm pretty sure (though not certain!) that this is not what Heaven will be like. The book of Revelation gives us a good idea of what Heaven will be like: angels and saints praising God with song and prayer. St. Paul tells us in 1 Corinthians 13 that love is what remains in the end, so Heaven is a place of endlessly loving God. The funeral liturgy uses language similar to our opening prayer for this day of Advent, calling it a banquet of eternal life. At a funeral Mass, we pray that God will grant the person a place at the eternal banquet of God's children. If you ask me what I think Heaven will be like, informed by the teaching of the saints and tradition, I believe that it will be an eternal Mass, an eternal eucharistic celebration. What we celebrate here

on earth every day at Holy Mass is a participation in and a foreshadowing of what is to come.

Our Advent prayer today begins with the words, "Prepare our hearts, we pray, O Lord." This is an acknowledgement that God begins our preparation. We prepare our hearts in so far as we cooperate with what God is doing and accomplishing. The prayer speaks of the banquet of eternal life. What we are asking of God is that He prepare our hearts so that we may be worthy of the banquet of eternal life. Again, it is the realization that we are unworthy, and it is only by the divine power of God that we become worthy. At the eucharistic banquet here on earth we pray these words, "Lord I am not worthy ..." It is God who says the word, invites us to the banquet, and allows us to receive that heavenly nourishment. The Eucharist that we receive at Mass comes from the hand of God, who has guided the creative action of the world, allowing wheat to grow, empowering farmers to harvest, and enabling vendors to make the host, which becomes the heavenly nourishment that we receive in the Eucharist.

Reflection Questions

1. Do you reflect on your worthiness or unworthiness of receiving Holy Communion? Do you examine your conscience to determine if you are conscious of grave sin and need sacramental Confession first?

    _____

    _____

    _____

    _____

2. What ways do you prepare for Mass? Is there any preparation on your part, or do you just show up? What could you do to prepare for Mass?

    _____

    _____

    _____

    _____

3. What is your attitude about Mass? Do you find it
    enriching or boring? What needs to change in you to
    better appreciate this heavenly gift?

    _____

    _____

    _____

    _____

THURSDAY OF THE
FIRST WEEK OF ADVENT

TODAY'S COLLECT

Stir up your power, O Lord,
and come to our help with mighty strength,
that what our sins impede
the grace of your mercy may hasten.

One of the key figures of Advent is John the Baptist, whose mission was to prepare the way of the Lord. He did this though a baptism of repentance. Repentance was a common theme throughout the Old Testament, that God's holy people had strayed, and prophets would call them back. People stray through sin. Unfortunately, sin is still around us today. And we are sinners. Some people are more aware of their sinfulness than others.

Today our Advent prayer focuses on God coming to our help with His mighty strength and mercy to overcome what our sins impede. Sin can hold us back in our relationship with God. Often, when a person falls into a habitual sin, they will stop praying and having recourse to God. The sin that they have committed might make them feel unworthy of God and unable to approach His throne of grace. Sin has the power to hold us back, but the good news of the Incarnation of Jesus and His coming as man is that sin doesn't have to hold that power any longer

because there is mercy, forgiveness, and redemption. His mercy hastens to us in the Sacrament of Reconciliation. If there is any gift that God wants to give you this Advent and Christmas, it is the gift of mercy and a new beginning. God has already given the gift; all we need to do is ask for it. If you no longer want to be impeded by sin, you know what you have to do.

Reflection Questions

1. When is the last time that you celebrated the Sacrament of Reconciliation? If it has been a long time, why don't you celebrate it more frequently? Is it because of inconvenient times it is offered or a fear of confessing your sins?

_____

_____

_____

_____

2. Is there a particular sin in your life that is impeding you right now?

_____

_____

_____

_____

3. Can you envision a life without a particular sin? Does ridding yourself of that sin bring you a greater sense of peace?

_____

_____

_____

Friday of the
First Week of Advent

Stir up your power, we pray, O Lord, and come,
that with you to protect us,
we may find rescue
from the pressing dangers of our sins,
and with you to set us free,
we may be found worthy of salvation.

In the storms we face in life, we look for a place of protection and shelter. If there is a tornado, a basement is the best place to be. If there is a hurricane, people will flee their home to find safety, or they will do everything that they can to protect their dwelling with exterior forces. A child runs to the arms of a parent when in trouble to find protection. In the spiritual life, we need protection too. It is protection from the evil one, who is compared to a lion prowling about in 1 Peter 5:8. When the lion is near, where do you find protection?

Our Advent prayer today asks the Lord to come and protect us. One of the surest places we can find the Lord's protection is within the Church. In every Catholic Church there is a tabernacle, and this is where we can run. If you are blessed to have an adoration chapel nearby, praying before the monstrance is also a powerful place of protection. When I have hit rock bottom at certain points, it is to Jesus in the Eucharist that I have run to find help and protection. Every

time that I have run to the Lord, after a time of prayer before
the Blessed Sacrament, I have received the strength to face
what was before me. St. Bernard of Clairvaux would recom-
mend running to Our Lady in trials and tribulations and
finding shelter and protection under her mantle. The saints
also serve a protective role when it comes to facing temptation. A saint like St. Benedict and his medal can protect one
against evil and the pressing dangers of sin. When you need
spiritual protection, remember where and to whom you
should go.

Reflection Questions

1. Have you found protection from God before in the Church at a time of crisis?

_____

_____

_____

_____

2. How do you pray in a moment of danger? What words do you pray?

_____

_____

_____

_____

3. Who provides you spiritual shelter?

_____

_____

_____

_____

Saturday of the
First Week of Advent

*O God, who sent your Only Begotten Son into this world
to free the human race from its ancient enslavement,
bestow on those who devoutly await him
the grace of your compassion from on high,
that we may attain the prize of true freedom.*

ary devoutly awaited the coming of the Christ Child. There are really three advents in Mary's life. The first is the long advent of the Jewish people. God promised a Messiah. The people waited, year after year, decade after decade, century after century. God is faithful and would one day fulfill that promise. And He did! Mary, as a chosen daughter of Israel, waited along with the Jewish people for the promised One. After the announcement made by the archangel Gabriel, Mary had a nine-month advent in which she waited to see the long-awaited Savior. The third advent of Mary's life was after the Ascension of Jesus and her waiting to be with the Lord again in Heaven.

Quite beautifully our Advent prayer today speaks to Jesus setting free humans from their ancient enslavement. This ancient enslavement is to the sin brought about by our parents Adam and Eve. It was because of this ancient enslavement that the whole world from generation to generation awaited the one who would correct everything.

There would be a new Adam and a new Eve. Mary, as the New Eve, devoutly awaited Jesus' coming. I can only imagine that she knew the Scriptures of the Old Testament that pertained to her and to this promised child. She devoutly waited, meditating on the Word of God. During this Advent season, we wait alongside Mary in the final weeks of her pregnancy. As we wait, let us do so devoutly so that we might receive God's grace and attain the heavenly prize.

Reflection Questions

1. How are you devoutly awaiting Jesus's coming? (One way is by praying through and reflecting on the Advent Collects.)

   _____

   _____

   _____

   _____

2. How well do you know the Old Testament passages referring to the Incarnation?

   _____

   _____

   _____

   _____

3. How do you imagine Mary devoutly awaited the coming
   and birth of Jesus?

   _____

   _____

   _____

Second Sunday
of Advent

*Almighty and merciful God,
may no earthly undertaking hinder those
who set out in haste to meet your Son,
but may our learning of heavenly wisdom
gain us admittance to his company.*

dvent is about setting out in haste to meet Christ, the Lord. This concept comes from Scripture and those who waited and were ready compared to those who were unprepared and not ready. Jesus teaches many parables about preparation and readiness. One of the ways that we ready ourselves is by learning. Today's Advent prayer draws our attention to the learning of heavenly wisdom.

There are many ways that we learn heavenly wisdom. It is true that God can impart His wisdom to us and that we can arrive at knowledge and understanding. Sitting in the presence of Jesus in the Eucharist can be an occasion of receiving heavenly wisdom too. Sometimes, I've prayed asking God to teach me a lesson or show me something. When I pray the Rosary, I ask Our Lady to bring me to meditate on something that I had never considered before. Sometimes she does! Besides prayer and open disposition in prayer, we often need to do something to learn and gain wisdom. We cannot expect to know the Word of God if we don't listen to the Scriptures at

Mass or open a Bible in our homes. The Scriptures are a place of heavenly wisdom. We cannot expect to know what the Bible is trying to communicate to us if we don't avail ourselves of some additional resource, such as a Bible study or a scriptural commentary. If I want to gain heavenly wisdom, I might need to do some spiritual reading. The saints were wise teachers. Though they lived many years removed from us, their powerful words are still teaching those who read them today.

Our Advent prayer today also asked God to let no earthly undertaking hinder us. We are busy people. A lot is expected and demanded of us. Sometimes these earthly undertakings are vying for our time and attention and might distract us from God. This Advent, we can choose to make learning heavenly wisdom a regular part of our lives.

Reflection Questions

1. How have you tried to learn heavenly wisdom?

   _____

   _____

   _____

   _____

2. What earthly undertakings distract you from heavenly goals?

   _____

   _____

   _____

   _____

3. Have you been a student of the saints and their writings? If not, is there a saint whose writings you would like to read?

_____

_____

_____

_____

Monday of the Second Week of Advent

TODAY'S COLLECT

*May our prayer of petition
rise before you, we pray, O Lord,
that, with purity unblemished,
we, your servants, may come, as we desire,
to celebrate the great mystery
of the Incarnation of your Only Begotten Son.*

hen a man studies in the seminary to be a priest, one of the courses that he will take is a Mass practicum. When I took the class, each week we recorded ourselves with a partner, celebrating and serving at Mass. We practiced using incense and incensing the altar, a beautiful symbol of what our opening prayer begins with today, our prayer of petition rising before the majesty of God. Our teacher was very emphatic when it came to a few things. The one thing that he was adamant about was that after the priest says or sings "The mystery of faith," he should be silent. He does not say, "We proclaim Your death O Lord ..." along with the faithful. Our teacher cited two reasons. First, the word for "mystery" means to be reduced to silence. The literal proclamation on the part of the priest means to be silent. The rubrics of the missal also say that the people say or sing the acclamation. The second reason he cited was that as a priest at the altar, you can behold the mystery of faith right in front

of you — that bread and wine became the Body, Blood, Soul, and Divinity of Jesus.

Today our Advent prayer says, "to celebrate the great mystery of the Incarnation of your Only Begotten Son." Our advent preparation leads to celebration of a great mystery. If we take the meaning of mystery to be reduced to silence seriously, we can ask: This Advent, has the mystery we are preparing for reduced you to silence? Jesus, the second Person of the Blessed Trinity, will be born of Mary and enter human existence. The heavenly realm will collide with the earthly world. God becomes an infant. God cries. God nurses at Mary's breast. Today, allow the great mystery of God becoming man take over your thought and meditation.

Reflection Questions

1. What does it mean to you that God became man?

_____

_____

_____

_____

2. Do some of the realities of our Faith ever reduce you to silence? If yes, what have you wondered and pondered over?

_____

_____

_____

_____

3. What Advent petition do you want to raise before the Lord's throne? What is the Advent grace for which you are asking?

_____

_____

_____

_____

TUESDAY OF THE SECOND WEEK OF ADVENT

Today's Collect

*O God, who have shown forth your salvation
to all the ends of the earth,
grant, we pray,
that we may look forward in joy
to the glorious Nativity of Christ.*

As a pastor and as a podcast host, I like to ask people, What are you looking forward to? Looking ahead is something that gives us great joy and hope. It could be a person looking forward to a vacation because they need time to decompress and enjoy life. You could be looking forward to having a few moments to get caught up on things that you have fallen behind on. You could look forward to something being over. For me, there have been times when looking forward was the only thing that got me through the day, week, or month. This might be how you feel on this Advent day: "I look forward to Christmas because things will slow down."

Today, our Advent prayer asks God to help us to look forward in joy to the glorious Nativity of Christ. What about Christmas are you looking forward to? Some people look forward to watching holiday movies, be it classics or new ones released on whatever streaming service or channel. Hopefully you are looking forward to being together

with family over Christmas. There are a lot of things in the worldly sense that we can look forward to, and that is great, but what about the spiritual sense? Are you looking forward to Christmas Mass? Are you looking forward to praying at the manger scene? If you don't know what you are looking for spiritually, ask God to show you what to look forward to when it comes to celebrating Jesus's birth.

Reflection Questions

1. Where is joy lacking in your life right now, and what can you do to change it?

_____

_____

_____

_____

2. What secular joy are you looking forward to regarding Christmas?

_____

_____

_____

_____

3. What spiritual joy are you looking forward to with Christ's Nativity?

_____

_____

_____

_____

WEDNESDAY OF THE SECOND WEEK OF ADVENT

*Almighty God, who command us
to prepare the way for Christ the Lord,
grant in your kindness, we pray,
that no infirmity may weary us
as we long for the comforting presence
of our heavenly physician.*

esus was a healer. Right now, think of one of the healing stories during Jesus' public ministry. Better yet, look up the story in your Bible and read it. My favorite healing story of Jesus revolves around Bartimaeus, a blind man on the side of the road. What fascinates me about his story is that as a blind man, someone had to tell him about Jesus and that Jesus was coming down the road. I love Jesus' question to Bartimaeus because the God of the universe, who knows everything asks him, What do you want me to do for you? I am moved by Jesus opening Bartimaeus's eyes and that Bartimaeus becomes a follower of Jesus.

Today, our Advent prayer asks God to grant that no infirmity may weary us as we long for the comforting presence of our heavenly physician. For some people, infirmity does indeed weary them. Recent tests at the doctor's office show abnormalities and now they need further testing. They are worried about what their diagnosis and prognosis will be. If it isn't a medical issue, maybe it's a psychological, financial,

emotional, or spiritual issue that is wearying them. Jesus' coming as an infant led to His public ministry and His miracles of healing. He becomes our heavenly physician. He still heals today. Personally, I have witnessed God's healing power, especially through the intercession of Our Lady of Lourdes. I've seen cancer disappear, wounds healed, pain vanished. God offers us healing at every Mass and at every Confession. We pray for healing right before receiving Holy Communion: "Only say the word, and my soul shall be healed." On this Advent day, pray for the healing you need or the healing of someone you love. Prayer is powerful. Pray, so that the way for Christ the physician may be open to those who need His healing presence.

Reflection Questions

1. Are you in need of healing? Are you aware of what it is? If not, ask God to bring healing to wherever He knows you need it.

   _____

   _____

   _____

   _____

2. Do you believe that God can heal people today? Why or why not?

   _____

   _____

   _____

   _____

3. How are you going to pray for healing today?

_____

_____

_____

_____

Thursday of the
Second Week of Advent

Stir up our hearts, O Lord,
to make ready the paths
of your Only Begotten Son,
that through his coming,
we may be found worthy to serve you
with minds made pure.

hat is God asking you to do this Advent? Maybe it's better to ask, What is God wanting to accomplish in your life this Advent? or simply, How does God want to use you? These are questions that we have already thought about in these reflections, yet our Advent prayer today brings them back to our attention. As the prayer begins, we ask the Lord to stir up our hearts to make ready the path. In this prayer, we are telling God, "I am ready to make the path ready for You." He's going to stir our hearts, giving us this desire. He already has done that if we want to be honest with ourselves. How is God asking me to make ready His path? What could I do? I'm just one person. We can even doubt that we can make any difference at all. But we can. The Lord is counting on us to make ready the path of Jesus. John the Baptist had his heart stirred up to do just that. He knew by divine grace when to begin his baptism of repentance. For you to make ready the path can be simple. It could be just striving to live a virtuous life,

choosing humility over pride, joy over sadness, compliment-
ing over complaining. We can make ready the path by our
own actions so that we do not become an obstacle to someone
else on the path.

The other part of today's Advent prayer asks that we may
be found worthy to serve the Lord with minds made pure.
Serving God may or may not be something we think about
often. In some ways it is innate within us. We hope that we
are serving God by how we carry out our lives. That as we go
about our day, we are doing His will and thus serving Him.
We also might not consider serving the Lord often and by
not thinking of it have missed opportunities. How each person serves the Lord is going to look different for each person,
given their vocation and life. The most important thing is to
consciously decide to serve the Lord and look for opportunities every day.

Reflection Questions

1. Choose one way that you will make ready the path of
   the Lord for the rest of Advent.

   _____

   _____

   _____

   _____

2. Name a few ways that you believe that you serve the
   Lord. Are there other ways to serve Him?

   _____

   _____

   _____

   _____

3. Is your mind pure, or is it attached to many things?
   How difficult will it be for God to make your mind
   pure?

   _____

   _____

   _____

   _____

FRIDAY OF THE
SECOND WEEK OF ADVENT

TODAY'S COLLECT

Grant that your people, we pray, almighty God,
may be ever watchful
for the coming of your Only Begotten Son,
that, as the author of our salvation himself has taught us,
we may hasten, alert and with lighted lamps,
to meet him when he comes.

Jesus is a teacher. We know this from the Gospel. His favorite way of teaching was through parables. Today's Advent prayer draws our focus to the parable of the ten virgins, who are awaiting the return of the bridegroom. As the oil runs out of the lamps, some of the virgins go in search of more oil while those who were prepared are ready. When the five foolish virgins leave, the bridegroom returns and they miss him. You can read the parable in Matthew 25:1–13. The purpose of Jesus' teaching here is to tell us that we do not know the day or the hour that Jesus will come back. Isn't that the funny thing? Many people have tried to make predictions, but they have always been wrong. Jesus already told us that we won't know when, but we think that maybe we broke the code and figured it out.

Another lesson that Jesus teaches us is that we must always be ready. Christians have waited for nearly two thousand years for the Parousia, the return of Christ. It hasn't happened. We are still waiting. If Jesus does not return while

we are alive, He will come for us at the hour of our death when we face our own judgment. The spiritual question we must ask here is Am I ready to meet the Lord right now? Today's prayer asks that we may hasten, alert, and with lighted lamps, to meet Him when He comes. But for some people who live their lives indifferent to the teachings of God, they may not want to hasten or be alert. In fact, if they saw the Lord coming, maybe they would run away because they are not ready. A person who may not be ready is one who is conscious of mortal sin or unrepentant of their sins. It could be someone who has not forgiven their brother as Jesus wants. Some people are ready. Older people I visit with are ready for Jesus to come for them. They have lived their lives and tried to please Him and pray daily that He will bring them home to His kingdom. This is how Jesus wants us to live our lives right now. He doesn't want us to be ready when we are seventy or eighty but at whatever age we are right now. He wants us to be ready because we are living a godly life right now.

Reflection Questions

1. Are you ready for the coming of Jesus at the unexpected hour?

   _____

   _____

   _____

   _____

2. What would hold you back from running to meet with Jesus?

   _____

   _____

   _____

   _____

3. What is the first thing that you will say to Jesus?

_____

_____

_____

_____

SATURDAY OF THE SECOND WEEK OF ADVENT

May the splendor of your glory dawn in our hearts,
we pray, almighty God,
that all shadows of the night may be scattered
and we may be shown to be children of light
by the advent of your Only Begotten Son.

As December goes on, the nights come earlier. When Christmas arrives, as the Light of the World enters the world, the days will begin to become longer. It will be by a few seconds, which then add up into minutes. The long, dark days begin to take a toll on us. We might even notice a bit of sadness creeping in. Luckily, God is going to shatter the darkness of night that we are currently experiencing, and light will dawn in the morning.

Today's Collect asks God to scatter the shadows of night so that we might be children of light. There are metaphorical shadows of night in our life. The first shadow of night is sin. We have become children of darkness because of Original Sin, but through Jesus and the Paschal Mystery, we can become children of light. After the Fall, Adam and Eve hid in shame. Ask Jesus to scatter the shadow of shame that you might experience because of past sins. You have become a child of light because of Christ's mercy and forgiveness. He has taken that shame away. Another shadow of night might

be doubt. This is doubt around who God is and what God does for us. It is doubt that He loves us and is with us in everything we experience. God, scatter this darkness, so that I believe with my whole mind, heart, and soul.

Whatever darkness you are experiencing right now in your life, ask God to scatter the darkness and usher in a new dawn of grace and light.

Reflection Questions

1. Do you enjoy darkness or light? Do you like driving at night or during the day? Which do you prefer? What might your answer mean for your spiritual life and relationship with God?

_____

_____

_____

_____

2. What areas of darkness do you sense in your heart, soul, mind, or life right now? What are you hoping for when the darkness scatters and dawn comes?

_____

_____

_____

_____

3. What doubts do you experience that need to be quelled
   by the Lord?

   _____

   _____

   _____

   _____

THIRD SUNDAY
OF ADVENT

Today's Collect

O God, who see how your people
faithfully await the feast of the Lord's Nativity,
enable us, we pray,
to attain the joys of so great a salvation
and to celebrate them always
with solemn worship and glad rejoicing.

Children sing that popular Christmas carol, "Santa Claus Is Coming to Town." There are a few lines in it that might seem rather creepy by today's standards: "He sees you when you're sleeping, / He knows when you're awake, / He knows if you have been bad or good, / So be good for goodness sake." Given that the celebration of Santa Claus and St. Nick is contingent upon being classified as naughty or nice, the line speaks to Santa knowing our behavior.

When it comes to God, He does in fact see us when we are sleeping, and He knows when we are awake. He knows what we do when no one is looking, and He hears the conversations we have with others. It is the Lord God who wants us to be holy and virtuous. Today's Collect reminds us that God sees us: "O God, who see how your people faithfully await the feast of the Lord's Nativity." God sees you right now as you read this book and meditate on the Incarnation, faithfully awaiting the coming of Christmas. He sees you in

line for Confession, and Jesus is there in the priest, *in persona Christi*, when you confess your sins. He sees you at adoration because you are adoring the very God who comes to us at Christmas as an infant. Your Advent waiting, prayer, and preparation are seen by God.

As we faithfully await the feast of the Lord's Nativity, we do so with solemn worship and glad rejoicing. We attend Mass, praying and praising God with the gathered community. We rejoice in what God has done, is doing, and will continue to do during these Advent days. As you worship and rejoice, know that God sees you and delights in what you are doing to prepare for the coming feasts.

Reflection Questions

1. What do you think God thinks of your Advent preparation? Is He pleased or do you think He knows you could do better?

_____

_____

_____

_____

2. What could you do in this second half of Advent to better prepare and wait for Christmas?

_____

_____

_____

_____

3. How do I characterize my worship of God? Is it solemn?
   Is it marked by joy?

_____

_____

_____

_____

MONDAY OF THE
THIRD WEEK OF ADVENT

Incline a merciful ear to our cry, we pray, O Lord,
and, casting light on the darkness of our hearts,
visit us with the grace of your Son.

When you and I were children, we were afraid of the dark. We were afraid of monsters that were hiding in the closet or under our bed. We needed a comforting presence, like a parent, to turn the lights on and tell us that there was nothing to fear to set our minds at ease. With them, we looked for the monsters and found none. In a spiritual sense, we also should be afraid of the darkness within our hearts. That darkness can be caused by present sins or sins from our past that linger in the dark, haunting us. The good news is that Jesus has come to shine light into these dark areas. He came so that we wouldn't be afraid of the dark any longer.

Sometimes we remain in the darkness because we have adjusted to it. Go into a restaurant with mood lighting. It takes a few minutes, but your eyes will adjust. At other times, when we are in the darkness, the light hurts our eyes when turned on. This might happen in the spiritual life. A person could have lived in darkness for so long, but a homily, book,

or podcast confronted that darkness and shined light into their life. This is what our Advent prayer today could mean by the visitation of the grace of Jesus. At first, when the light shines in a dark area of sin and we know we must change, it can hurt, and maybe we resist it for a while. Choosing to embrace the light and leave the darkness behind will make all the difference. Think of some of the people who were visited by Jesus in the Gospels: the woman caught in adultery, for example. She was in darkness of sexual sin, but Jesus comes, shines light into her life, saves her life, and tells her to sin no more. Certainly, her past remaining with her might frighten her, but there is the promise of a new day because of what Jesus obtained for her.

From our darkness, we cry out to the Lord, hear us, cast Your light, and bring us Your grace!

Reflection Questions

1. Can you name the darkness of your heart?

   _____

   _____

   _____

   _____

2. Have you ever had an experience where something that a saint or author wrote, the words of Jesus, or the *Catechism* challenged you? Did you allow these words to stay with you?

   _____

   _____

   _____

   _____

3. What grace do you specifically want the Lord to bring
   you today?

   _____

   _____

   _____

   _____

TUESDAY OF THE
THIRD WEEK OF ADVENT

O God, who through your Only Begotten Son
have made us a new creation,
look kindly, we pray,
on the handiwork of your mercy,
and at your Son's coming
cleanse us from every stain of the old way of life.

N ever wear white if you plan on eating spaghetti. That's good advice, isn't it? We have all been there. You are wearing your nicest clothes, eating a gourmet meal, and food falls off of your fork and now your shirt is stained. It happens, too, when we spill coffee and it stains. If you are lucky, you might have a Tide pen with you and can quickly blot it out. If not, you will treat the stain before washing. At times, maybe the stain doesn't fully remove, and there is a little remnant of the blotch. Many people won't see it unless they are looking for it, but you know that the spot is there, and it will bother you. You will probably end up cycling the shirt out of your wardrobe rotation, and it will remain there until your next purge.

Our Advent prayer today emphasizes that Jesus' coming can cleanse us from every stain of our old way of life. We all have the events of the past. Whatever has happened or whatever we have done will bother us. The hope is that as we continue to become a better follower and disciple of Jesus,

the ways of our past will be behind us, and we will only focus on the present moment and the future. Becoming a follower of Jesus has changed every part of my life—and yet, I still have dirty, stained laundry. But Jesus wants to remove the stains, spots, and blemishes by His blood. The old way of doing things has been usurped by the new way of living proposed by Jesus. As I decide to follow Jesus and live His teachings, that old way will begin to disappear. Bad habits will be eliminated, and godly ways will take over. We will still have memories of these sinful decisions, but by prayer and the sacraments, we ask Jesus to remove these memories and purify our minds, so that these stains of my old life no longer have to linger and haunt me. Jesus has come to remove the stains of our old life and calls us to a better life of knowing, following, and loving Him. Rejoice, because you have become a new creation.

Reflection Questions

1. Can you name some of the stains caused by your old way of life?

   _____

   _____

   _____

   _____

2. How have you sensed a difference in your life because of the new way that comes with believing in and following Jesus?

   _____

   _____

   _____

   _____

3. What are aspects of the Lord's "handiwork of mercy"?

_____

_____

_____

_____

WEDNESDAY OF THE
THIRD WEEK OF ADVENT

Grant, we pray, almighty God,
that the coming solemnity of your Son
may bestow healing upon us in this present life
and bring us the rewards of life eternal.

Over the years I have been an on-again, off-again runner. Over a decade ago, I ran my longest race: a half marathon. Now, I am lucky to get two or three miles in a few times each week. As a runner, one of my favorite Scripture passages comes from 2 Timothy 4:7: "I have fought the good fight, I have finished the race, I have kept the faith." This Scripture passage is sometimes used for funerals, analogizing, as St. Paul does, life on earth to a race, and what awaits us is a crown of righteousness.

What is the point of exercising or running? I need to do it to burn calories and to maintain or lose weight. There are lots of added benefits too. There is an endorphin release, and I feel better about myself and everything going on in life. Sometimes a person might run and consequently reward themselves once they reach a certain goal. When I was trying to lose weight, when I would hit a certain plateau, I would have some reward. If I hit this weight, I am going to wear this shirt that I haven't been able to fit in. If I get to a certain

weight, I will enjoy a dessert since I have been denying myself. I have found this reward mentality helpful.

Life is a race. Because you are a believer, you know what
awaits you. The Gospels are filled with promises. In John 6,
Jesus promises eternal life to those who eat His Body and
drink His Blood. Because I receive the Eucharist, practice my
faith, and follow the teachings of Jesus, I know what awaits
me. Our yearly observance of Advent is a reminder that Jesus
was born to save me from my sins and open the gates of
Heaven. His coming brings me healing. His coming helps
me anticipate the rewards of keeping the Faith and fighting
the good fight, that one day I will live with God forever in
Heaven. Be faithful now in this present life so that you will
receive the reward of eternal life.

Reflection Questions

1. How has reward-focused achievement aided you in your life?

_____

_____

_____

_____

2. What are some spiritual goals that you have, and how can you attain them?

_____

_____

_____

_____

3. What type of healing do you stand most in need of right
   now?

   _____

   _____

   _____

   _____

Thursday of the
Third Week of Advent

Unworthy servants that we are, O Lord,
grieved by the guilt of our deeds,
we pray that you may gladden us
by the saving advent of your Only Begotten Son.

It is unfortunate, but there is a negative phrase associated with being a Catholic Christian in mainstream culture. Some people refer to "Catholic guilt." I had an individual tell me once that she was "over" feeling guilty about everything and looked for spiritual fulfillment outside the Church. That saddened me. This Catholic guilt occurs because of choices that we have made, things we have failed to do, or sins we have committed. The guilt that overcomes a person because of their sinfulness might even lead them to question if they are a good Catholic. Guilt is a reminder to us of how we need to change and perhaps of our unwillingness to confront our weaknesses, temptations, and sins.

It is spiritually healthy for us to be grieved by the guilt of our deeds. That guilt leads us to the confessional line so that we can seek the mercy and forgiveness of God. At times, God shows us sins from our past so that we can grieve our infidelity to His commands and make a conscious decision to change our ways. We grieve over our sins so that we can

experience joy and relief through mercy and forgiveness. Every time I go to Confession, weighed down by sinfulness, I walk out the door feeling lighter because God has removed that weight of sin.

Consider any number of people in the Gospels who came to Jesus. Let's take for example the woman caught in adultery. She was grieved by the guilt of her deeds, but Jesus' forgiveness was powerful, and she was told to go and sin no more. What gladness she must have experienced. Many wanted to stone her. Jesus rescued her, forgave her, and set her on a new path. Jesus' birth gives way to His public ministry and forgiveness of sins. His advent allows us during this Advent to be forgiven and gladdened by His mercy. We have grieved because of our sins, but Jesus wishes to turn that grief into joy. It's time to let go of our grief and guilt and to be gladdened by the grace of Jesus.

Reflection Questions

1. Have you experienced "Catholic guilt" before? What helped you to let go of it?

_____

_____

_____

_____

2. Does guilt provide any element of positivity for you?

_____

_____

_____

_____

3. Have you experienced a weight being lifted when you experienced the mercy of Jesus in the Sacrament of Reconciliation?

_____

_____

_____

_____

FRIDAY OF THE THIRD WEEK OF ADVENT

TODAY'S COLLECT

May your grace, almighty God,
always go before us and follow after,
so that we, who await with heartfelt desire
the coming of your Only Begotten Son,
may receive your help both now and in the life to come.

One of my favorite quotes from Bl. Solanus Casey is, "Thank God ahead of time." What he is saying is that as we pray for an intention, thank God ahead of His action. It is a way of anticipating that God is going to act. It does mean that we might be thanking God ahead of time for answering us in a way that we did not expect or want. It indicates our openness to God's will.

Our Advent prayer today asks, "May your grace ... always go before us and follow after." God's grace goes before us and follows after us. This is a complex prayer. It's hard for us to grasp its significance. *May your grace always go before us.* As I rise at the beginning of the day, Lord, may Your grace go before me. When taking a phone call, Lord may Your grace go before me. We want His grace to go before us so that we are always cooperating and responding to the movement of His grace and accomplishing His will. We want His grace to follow after too. Think about the conversations that you have with people. May God's grace follow after you, not

only for you, but for that person with whom you interacted. God's grace might go before me, opening my heart and mind to help someone in need that I encounter, and His grace follows after, helping me to be grateful for what I have and for the beneficiary in the goodness that he received.

The St. Patrick's Breastplate prayer also might help give an image to this Advent prayer: "Christ with me, Christ before me, Christ behind me, Christ in me, Christ beneath me, Christ above me, Christ on my right, Christ on my left." The coming of Jesus at Christmas assures me that Christ accompanies me throughout my life. He sends His grace ahead of me and after me. I just need His help to identify and know the working of grace so that I might be moved to thank Him before, during, and after.

Reflection Questions

1. How have you noticed God's grace going before you or following after you?

_____

_____

_____

_____

2. Have you ever thanked God ahead of time?

_____

_____

_____

_____

3. What does the prayer mean when it speaks of receiving
   God's help in the life to come?

   _____

   _____

   _____

   _____

Fourth Sunday
of Advent

Pour forth, we beseech you, O Lord,
your grace into our hearts,
that we, to whom the Incarnation of Christ your Son
was made known by the message of an Angel,
may by his Passion and Cross
be brought to the glory of his Resurrection.

oday's Advent prayer should sound familiar to devout Catholics because it's the closing prayer of the Angelus. Whenever I talk about the reference, the image I always have in mind, besides the angel's announcement to Mary, is the painting of Jean-François Millet called *The Angelus*, which depicts a farmer and his wife praying in the field. Way off in the distance, you can see a church in the background. A viewer of the painting is left to imagine that the church bells are ringing at six, noon, or six, and the devoted couple bows their head in prayer.

A lot of our Marian devotion in the Church is meant to mimic the liturgical life of the Church. For example, the Rosary of 150 Hail Mary prayers was to resemble the monk's prayer of the 150 psalms during the Liturgy of the Hours. The Angelus, prayed three times a day, in the morning, at midday, and in the evening, mirrors the liturgical life of monks who pray their Lauds, Sext, and Vespers. It is customary to genuflect during the third versicle and response—"and

the Word became flesh and dwelt among us." This line comes to us from the prologue of St. John's Gospel and emphasizes the Incarnation, that God became man in the birth of the divine Son. The gesture of genuflection mirrors the Church's action on Christmas Eve and Day during the Nicene Creed at Mass, when the priest and congregants are instructed by the missal to kneel at the words "and became incarnate of the Virgin Mary" rather than the customary profound bow at every other Sunday Mass throughout the year. The Angelus is prayed throughout the year, except for the fifty days of Easter when it is replaced by the Regina Caeli.

The Angelus prayer is a reminder to us that Christ came to earth for our salvation. If you want the grace of Christmas to endure throughout the year, pray the Angelus. By meditating on Christ's Incarnation with the Angelus, you will be invoking Mary's intercession, asking God to pour His grace into your heart, and praying for your eventual glorification one day, in death, by Christ's Resurrection. The Angelus is a most fitting Advent and Christmas prayer, and one that helps us throughout the year never to forget the mystery and gift of what Jesus accomplished.

Reflection Questions

1. Do you have set times when you pray throughout the day?

   _____

   _____

   _____

   _____

2. Do you set alarms to remind you to pray?

   _____

   _____

   _____

   _____

3. What would hold you back or prevent you from praying
   the Angelus?

   _____

   _____

   _____

   _____

DECEMBER 17

O God, Creator and Redeemer of human nature,
who willed that your Word should take flesh
in an ever-virgin womb,
look with favor on our prayers,
that your Only Begotten Son,
having taken to himself our humanity,
may be pleased to grant us a share in his divinity.

When we speak about Mary, we will often emphasize her role as Mother or Queen. In common language related to Our Lady, we will often call her the Blessed Virgin Mary or Virgin Mary. As a Church, we believe in the tripartite (threefold) virginity of Mary: before, during, and after the birth of Christ (pre-, in, post-partum).

The three-fold virginity of Mary has been a part of our tradition since the late 300s and was affirmed by different Church councils in 553, 649, and 1215. There are scholarly opinions that Mary had taken a vow of virginity while she was a child, and that even though she was married to Joseph, she intended to keep that vow. Mary attests to her virginity before the birth of Christ with her response to the angel, "How can this be since I have had no relations with a man?" (see Luke 1:34). Her virginity after Christ's birth can be explained, but certain references in the Gospels, such as referring to Jesus as her first-born son, Joseph not knowing Mary until Jesus was

born, and references to the brothers and sisters of the Lord, complicate matters. With the help of St. Jerome, we know that the brothers and sisters of the Lord are cousins or close relatives, and later references in the Gospels seem to corroborate this. Mary's virginity during the birth of Christ deals with questions about the intactness of her virginity and pain in childbirth. It's a question that has been controversial theologically, so much so that the Congregation for the Doctrine of the Faith placed a moratorium on the debate.

Why does it matter? What value is this belief of the perpetual virginity of Mary besides being encouraging to those vowed to it in the Church? Why couldn't Mary have other children? St. Thomas Aquinas gives a handful of reasons for Mary's perpetual virginity after the birth of Jesus. He cites Jesus as the perfect offspring, the sacredness of Mary's womb, Mary's gratitude for the only begotten Son, and St. Joseph's respect for Mary's virginity and role in the extraordinary event of the Incarnation. Mary's perpetual virginity is something that the Church has held for centuries. In the Guadalupe apparition to St. Juan Diego, Mary tells him that she is ever-virgin. Our Advent prayer today draws our focus to the ever-virgin womb of Mary and moves us to gratitude because in her womb she bore the Son of the Eternal Father.

Reflection Questions

1. What questions are unresolved for you regarding Mary's perpetual virginity?

   _____

   _____

   _____

   _____

2. How does the perpetual virginity of Mary challenge or encourage you in your pursuit of virtue?

   _____

   _____

   _____

   _____

3. Which title or attribute do you use when referring or praying to Mary?

_____

_____

_____

_____

DECEMBER 18

Grant, we pray, almighty God,
that we, who are weighed down from of old
by slavery beneath the yoke of sin,
may be set free by the newness
of the long-awaited Nativity
of your Only Begotten Son.

The Church's liturgical cycle presents to us the same readings and same feasts throughout the year. You always know what you are going to get and what to expect. Every three years, the same Sunday Mass readings. The same Gospel every year. Even though there is the sameness and routine in the Church's life, there is still a newness to our experience. The way that I experience a Scripture passage is going to be different this year than last year because I'm more mature and have had more life experiences from which to draw. The Scriptures can speak to us in new ways even though they are familiar.

Today our Collect asks God to set us free by the newness of the long-awaited Nativity. It's the same Christmas every year. Jesus is wrapped in swaddling clothes and laid in a manger. We know the story. If you pray the Rosary, it's the subject of routine meditation during the third joyful mystery. Yet there is a newness to the Christmas mystery. For a mom who recently gave birth or the first-time father seeing

his child, there is a newness to Christmas, relating to Mary's pregnancy, and the wonder of Mary and Joseph as they saw Jesus for the very first time. A person who has been ridden with anxiety and has had it lifted recently will hear the words of the angel speaking of peace much differently. The long-awaited Nativity happened centuries ago. But there is a newness in celebrating it again this year. Jesus wants to do something special in your life this year. He brings freedom from sin and the past and promises a brighter tomorrow.

Reflection Questions

1. Imagine what it would be like for a person to hear the story of Jesus's birth for the very first time. What do you think would impress them the most?

   _____

   _____

   _____

   _____

2. Read Luke's account of Jesus's birth. It's been almost a whole year since you have read or heard this text! What stands out to you this year?

   _____

   _____

   _____

   _____

3. Has this Advent helped you transform your old way of
   life into a new way of life?

   _____

   _____

   _____

   _____

DECEMBER 19

O God, who through the child-bearing of the holy Virgin
graciously revealed the radiance of your glory to the world,
grant, we pray,
that we may venerate with integrity of faith
the mystery of so wondrous an Incarnation
and always celebrate it with due reverence.

As Catholics, we hold Mary in high esteem and honor. Our Protestant brothers and sisters don't quite understand it and sometimes think it might be too much, bordering on worship. Some fellow Catholics might not give Mary much consideration or thought. They don't pray the Rosary and don't get what the big deal is when it comes to her. The reason why we honor her so much is because of her role in salvation history. We esteem her because of what God did for her and how God used her. Of all the women that ever existed, He chose her, a virgin girl in Nazareth, to be the mother of the Savior of the world. As our Advent prayer says today, through Mary's childbearing she revealed God's radiance and glory to the world. Our Advent observance and preparation for Christmas is right alongside the time of Mary's childbearing, which brings us hope and salvation.

Our Advent preparation and celebration of Christmas should be marked by veneration and reverence of the mystery we commemorate. The mystery being that Jesus, who is

pre-existent with the Father, the second Person of the Trinity, dwells in the womb of Mary and becomes man. The fact that God became one like us in all things but sin is incomprehensible. Our Advent prayer encourages us to celebrate this mystery with due reverence. How can we do that? There is enough irreverence with people who destroy Nativity scenes, and some of the Christmas movies that are produced might not reverently celebrate the mystery of Christmas. Do you have a nativity scene set up? Each time you pass by it or look at it, this is a moment to pause and think of the Incarnation, celebrating it with due reverence. As you ponder over the manger scene, let it be a moment to think of that wonderful gift of Mary's childbearing and all that it entails, from God's choice of her to her cooperation in allowing the Word to become flesh.

Reflection Questions

1. How would you classify your devotion to Mary?

   _____

   _____

   _____

   _____

2. Do you honor her in ways similar to how believers and saints have done so throughout the centuries?

   _____

   _____

   _____

   _____

3. How can you give the proper respect and reverence to the mystery of Christmas as an individual or family?

_____

_____

_____

_____

DECEMBER 20

TODAY'S COLLECT

O God, eternal majesty, whose ineffable Word
the immaculate Virgin received through
the message of an Angel
and so became the dwelling-place of divinity,
filled with the light of the Holy Spirit,
grant, we pray, that by her example
we may in humility hold fast to your will.

Advent rightfully focuses on Jesus. It's all about preparing for His birth and return in glory. The Holy Spirit, though, has a role to play during Advent too. While the Annunciation and Visitation are celebrated in March and May respectively, during these Advent days, we read and reflect about these events as part of how the birth of Jesus Christ came about. The Holy Spirit played a pivotal role at these two events. At the Annunciation, the Holy Spirit dwelt within Mary, conceiving Jesus in her womb. The Holy Spirit prompted Mary to visit Elizabeth, and the Spirit prompted Elizabeth to declare Mary blessed among women and the mother of the Lord.

Just as Mary was a dwelling place of divinity, we can also become dwelling places of God's divinity. The Holy Spirit is with us by the power of our Baptism and Confirmation. The Holy Spirit has come to us with His gifts, and we strive to make use of them. The same Holy Spirit can inspire us in our words and actions. When difficult conversations need to

be had, the Holy Spirit can inspire us in what we should say. The Holy Spirit might also place on our hearts something that we should do and somewhere that we should go, so out of obedience to the Holy Spirit, we respond to these promptings after prayer and discernment. The Holy Spirit is also present at every Mass, by whose power the gifts of bread and wine become the Body and Blood of Jesus. Like Mary, Jesus can dwell in us by the power of the Holy Spirit through the Eucharist. Jesus dwells within us after Holy Communion. How different would I be as a Christian living in the world if I realized that I became a dwelling place of divinity? Such a realization would change my conversations, choices, and decisions. With the help of the Holy Spirit and Mary's examples, we can become receptive to the ineffable Word of God, who dwells among us.

Reflection Questions

1. How aware am I that God dwells in me at every Holy Communion?

_____

_____

_____

_____

2. Where do I need the light of the Holy Spirit to shine in my life right now?

_____

_____

_____

_____

3. What is the Holy Spirit revealing to me or how is the
   Holy Spirit leading/guiding me right now?

_____

_____

_____

_____

December 21

TODAY'S COLLECT

Hear in kindness, O Lord,
the prayers of your people,
that those who rejoice
at the coming of your Only Begotten Son in our flesh
may, when at last he comes in glory,
gain the reward of eternal life.

We pray to God all the time. We lift prayers of petition for people we love and those for whom we promise to pray. We offer prayers of gratitude to God for the many blessings that He has bestowed upon us. We ask Him for forgiveness. When we pray, God hears us. He listens to our prayers. He helps us in unimaginable ways. Sometimes we are unaware of God's provident grace at work in our lives, and other times it is very apparent.

I think of the Jewish people of long ago. They had been waiting year after year for the Almighty to send the promised Messiah. They prayed and waited. Through the Incarnation, God heard their prayers, and their wait was over. Many wouldn't realize this for a while. Mary was one of these people praying for the Messiah and waiting. God heard her prayer, chose her, and she was waiting, with the long-expected one in her womb for nine months, and then she gave birth and saw the one for whom her ancestors and she had prayed.

God heard the prayers of the aged Elizabeth and Zechariah, who for a long time desired a child. When all hope seemed lost, an angel announces to Zechariah the good news. Mary is told of it and visits her cousin. Together, these two women rejoice in God's answer to prayer.

In many ways, we are just like the people of long ago. We now are praying that Jesus will return and establish a new Heaven and a new earth. We are waiting just like they did. As we wait, we pray. And as we pray, God in His kindness hears our prayers. As we wait, we rejoice in His eventual return, when He comes at last.

Reflection Questions

1. When you pray, do you approach prayer with the belief that God hears you and will answer you?

   _____

   _____

   _____

   _____

2. Recall a time when God answered your prayer. How grateful were you? What did that do for your faith?

   _____

   _____

   _____

   _____

3. Have you ever meditated about Jesus' return in glory
   and what it will be like? If not, reread some of the
   Scripture passages that speak to this, like Matthew 25.

_____

_____

_____

_____

DECEMBER 22

TODAY'S COLLECT

O God, who, seeing the human race fallen into death,
willed to redeem it by the coming of your Only Begotten Son,
grant, we pray,
that those who confess his Incarnation with humble fervor
may merit his company as their Redeemer.

I love to people-watch. Sitting at a coffee shop, as I write this manuscript, I see the people around me and wonder about their stories and how God has been active in their lives. Airports are great for people-watching. Sometimes, as you see people in your day-to-day life, you are moved to compassion and pity for the person. The person who has ragged clothes, and you realize that they probably don't have many resources available to them. You see the person who has had a long-time disability, and your heart breaks for them and all that they have experienced.

God is a people-watcher. This is a God who is not indifferent to us. This is a God who cares about us and sees our actions. This is the God who saw Adam and Eve in the Garden after the Fall and sought them out and inquired about their actions. This is the God who saw people turning away from His ways and disobeying His commands.

Imagine what God sees as He looks at the world today, as He looks at you, and me, and everybody else on the

planet. He sees moral depravity. He sees our many sins. He sees how the human race has fallen into death time and again. The good news is that because He sent His Son so many years ago, He can raise from the dead those who have spiritually died. Today in your prayer, ask the Lord to look out into the world and to find the soul that is in most need of your prayers. Ask Him to use your prayers to bring them from the brink of spiritual death to new life. As God sees that person and hears your prayer, hopefully one day when we merit the company of Jesus in Heaven, He will introduce us to that person and tell you that your prayers on one Advent day secured this person's conversion and salvation.

Reflection Questions

1. Have you considered how your prayers can help a person at a desperate moment or a soul in Purgatory who is nearly ready to be delivered to eternity?

_____

_____

_____

_____

2. As the Lord sees the human race fallen into death, consider what He sees as He looks at you.

_____

_____

_____

_____

3. At the end of our lives, we pray to be found worthy of
   Heaven. What do you imagine it to be like to keep
   company with the Redeemer in eternity?

   _____

   _____

   _____

   _____

DECEMBER 23

Almighty ever-living God,
as we see how the Nativity of your Son
according to the flesh draws near,
we pray that to us, your unworthy servants,
mercy may flow from your Word,
who chose to become flesh of the Virgin Mary
and establish among us his dwelling,
Jesus Christ our Lord.

In Matthew 1:18, the evangelist writes, "Now the birth of Jesus Christ took place in this way." In these final days of Advent, the Church reads sequentially from the Gospels, leading us to the moment of His birth in Bethlehem. Through this reading of the Gospels and the different events before the birth of Jesus, we discover how the Nativity of Jesus draws nearer. In our own lived experience of these past days and today and tomorrow, we see how Christmas draws nearer. If you go to Mass, the Advent wreath candle from the first week is probably dwindling, and you wonder if it will even make it! One time, I witnessed an Advent wreath catch on fire from a shortened candle. If you have to go to the store before Christmas, either to shop for gifts or to get things that you need for your life, you will notice that Christmas is drawing nearer as the lines are getting longer. It seems that each Christmas, I go to a local shoe store to buy a new pair of shoes, and I have to wait in line because everybody else also had that idea. Christmas is drawing nearer. Christ will make His dwelling among us.

Christ's mercy is another sign to us of Christmas drawing nearer. If Confessions are offered today or tomorrow, there is bound to be a line. It is the realization of that for which we pray in today's prayer: mercy flowing from the Word. People seek out Confession because they want their lives to change. They believe in God's mercy and the transformative grace that Jesus offers. I am moved so often by the Word of God, which are the Scriptures, because it challenges me often to change my way of life and conform more closely to Christ. Hearing the words of the one we call The Word, Jesus, in the Gospels reminds me that I need forgiveness, and I am not living up to the ideal He proposes. As the Nativity of Jesus draws nearer, what I want is His mercy. What a gift that Jesus came to institute the sacraments that we have today and to reconcile the world with God by His death on the Cross, and the promise of everlasting life when He defeats death by the Resurrection.

Reflection Questions

1. Are you excited that Christmas is drawing nearer?

_____

_____

_____

_____

2. Do you wish that Advent was longer?

_____

_____

_____

_____

3. How will you maintain the spirit of Christmas in a
   world that celebrates it for one day, while the Church
   celebrates it for a few weeks?

   _____

   _____

   _____

   _____

DECEMBER 24

TODAY'S COLLECT

Come quickly, we pray, Lord Jesus,
and do not delay,
that those who trust in your compassion
may find solace and relief in your coming.

uring the Advent season we invite Jesus to come. We sing it. "O come divine Messiah." "O come, O come Emmanuel." Today our Advent prayer asks Jesus to "come quickly … and do not delay." This might not be your prayer. With it being the final hour before Christmas arrives and you having so much to do, you might not pray these words "come quickly" because you feel that you need more time. Some people have had their Christmas trees up for weeks, and maybe you are seizing this moment to put yours up today. We don't want Jesus to come quickly, because we still need to clean the house for guests or prepare Christmas dinner. We want Jesus to delay just a little while longer because we need to wrap Christmas presents that we'll be gifting over the next few days.

Advent always feels like it passes quickly, and we don't accomplish all that we had set out to do. Our days get busy with concerts and parties, and we keep saying, "I'll get to that tomorrow." Tomorrow didn't come and now Christmas

Eve is here. This procrastination happens not only with our Advent observances but in our spiritual lives too. Maybe I delay praying the Rosary from the morning to the evening, only to realize when I am in bed that my delay caused me to forget to pray today. As we close the door on this year's Advent and open the door for Christmas, maybe our final Advent prayer can be a reminder to seize every opportunity that we have to take advantage of the present moment. Jesus is coming quickly and will not delay. It would be best for us to make this our approach to daily living too. We always will think that we have more time. But one day there won't be any more time.

Do not delay in accepting the gift of what is today and what is being offered right now to us by God. Do not delay in celebrating the Sacrament of Reconciliation. Do not delay in reaching out and making amends. Do not delay in giving to someone in need. It is easy to delay, but it is better if we do not.

Reflection Questions

1. How have you procrastinated this Advent, and what is one thing that you want to accomplish today before Christmas begins?

_____

_____

_____

_____

2. What is one thing that you delayed doing in your life that you regretted afterward?

_____

_____

_____

_____

3. What grace of Advent do you hope will remain with you in the weeks ahead?

_____

_____

_____

_____

PROPERS OF SAINTS

DECEMBER 8
IMMACULATE CONCEPTION

TODAY'S COLLECT

O God, who by the Immaculate
Conception of the Blessed Virgin
prepared a worthy dwelling for your Son,
grant, we pray,
that, as you preserved her from every stain
by virtue of the Death of your Son, which you foresaw,
so, through her intercession,
we, too, may be cleansed and admitted to your presence.

The Immaculate Conception is one of the most misunderstood Marian teachings. Since this feast day falls a few weeks before Christmas, many people wrongly associate it with being the conception of Jesus. If that was the case, it was a super fast pregnancy. The conception of Jesus is celebrated as the Annunciation on March 25. The Immaculate Conception celebrates what God did for Mary, preserving her from Original Sin at the moment of her conception in the womb of St. Anne. Mary's birthday or nativity is celebrated nine months from today, on September 8.

What fascinates me about the Immaculate Conception is that in virtue of what God did for Mary, she had to be different than any other child. Preserved from every stain of sin by the death of Jesus, which would occur decades later, she was sinless. I wonder if people knew that Mary was special the way that people know if a child is a savant or prodigy.

In the struggles that we face with sin, vice, and temptation, Mary as the sinless one can intercede and pray for us. Her prayers can help us overcome sin and temptation and grow in virtue. As a mother washes the face of her child, Mary obtains cleansing for us. Just as a mother wants what is good for her child, Mary prays that we will be worthy of being in the presence of God. Turn to Mary and ask her to help you as you live your life as a disciple.

Reflection Questions

1. Mary is a remedy to what is happening in our lives. If you struggle with doubt, Mary can pray for you to have faith. If you hate, Mary can help you love. Name your vice and ask her to pray for the corresponding virtue.

   _____

   _____

   _____

   _____

2. What do you think that the childhood of Mary was like?

   _____

   _____

   _____

   _____

3. Do you believe that Mary is in your corner and has your
   back?

   _____

   _____

   _____

   _____

December 12
Our Lady of Guadalupe

Today's Collect

O God, Father of mercies,
who placed your people under the singular protection
of your Son's most holy Mother,
grant that all who invoke the Blessed Virgin of Guadalupe,
may seek with ever more lively faith
the progress of peoples in the ways of justice and of peace.

Our Lady played a very special role in the life of St. Juan Diego, the visionary of the Guadalupe apparitions. Our Lady addressed him so tenderly, calling him her little Juan Diego. When it comes to these apparitions of Our Lady, it is God who sends her with a message. God desired the conversion of a people who had gone astray, and Our Lady would touch their hearts and bring them back. Many conversions and Baptisms resulted following the apparitions of Our Lady of Guadalupe.

She said these words: "Let not your heart be disturbed.... Am I not here, who am your Mother? Are you not under my protection? Am I not your health? Are you not happily within my fold? What else do you wish? Do not grieve nor be disturbed by anything." These words are so touching, and they echo the Gospel. Jesus so often repeated these words, "Do not be afraid." Mary, who heard these words from the archangel, says them to Juan Diego and repeats them in many of her apparitions.

Devotion to Our Lady of Guadalupe is widespread. People will gather in Mexico City outside the basilica and sing to Our Lady, serenading her with prayer and song. This is the mother who promised to protect and hear her children. How is your devotion to Mary? Do you ask for her prayers often? Mary is a key figure of Advent, and we can journey with her during these days leading up to Christmas. If you have a Marian devotion, keep journeying with Mary. If you don't have one, maybe this is the moment to begin in a simple way with the Hail Mary. As you begin or deepen your devotion, you will experience what Our Lady promised, her prayers and protection. And your fears will disappear.

Reflection Questions

1. What are the characteristics of your devotion to Mary right now? Do you have a statue or picture of her? Do you pray her Rosary?

   _____

   _____

   _____

   _____

2. Have you ever looked at the image of Our Lady of Guadalupe? If not, look it up and see what she looks like. This image was impressed on a tilma and is still viewed and venerated today.

   _____

   _____

   _____

   _____

3. What prayer petition do you want Our Lady to pray for today?

_____

_____

_____

_____

ABOUT THE AUTHOR

FR. EDWARD LOONEY WAS ordained a priest in 2015 for the Diocese of Green Bay. In addition to a bachelor of philosophy, a baccalaureate in sacred theology (S.T.B.), and a master of divinity, he holds a licentiate in sacred theology (S.T.L.) from the University of St. Mary of the Lake-Mundelein Seminary. Fr. Looney specializes in Marian theology, having authored numerous works on Mary, including *A Lenten Journey with Mother Mary* and *How They Love Mary: 28 Life-Changing Stories of Devotion to Our Lady*, available from Sophia Institute Press. He is a past president of the Mariological Society of America, currently serving as the Society's secretary, and continues to research, reflect, and write about Mary. Fr. Looney is a popular media personality, podcast host, and contributor to online and print publications, like *Living Faith*. His interests include the Blessed Virgin, sainthood causes, shrines, and film/television.

COMING IN JANUARY 2025

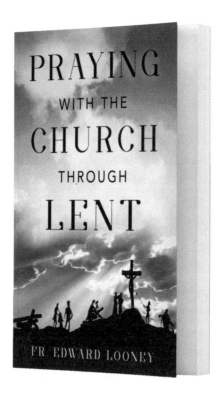

PRAYING
WITH THE CHURCH
THROUGH LENT
by Fr. Edward Looney

Sophia Institute

SOPHIA INSTITUTE IS A nonprofit institution that seeks to nurture the spiritual, moral, and cultural life of souls and to spread the gospel of Christ in conformity with the authentic teachings of the Roman Catholic Church.

Sophia Institute Press fulfills this mission by offering translations, reprints, and new publications that afford readers a rich source of the enduring wisdom of mankind.

Sophia Institute also operates the popular online resource CatholicExchange.com. *Catholic Exchange* provides world news from a Catholic perspective as well as daily devotionals and articles that will help readers to grow in holiness and live a life consistent with the teachings of the Church.

In 2013, Sophia Institute launched Sophia Institute for Teachers to renew and rebuild Catholic culture through service to Catholic education. With the goal of nurturing the spiritual, moral, and cultural life of souls, and an abiding respect for the role and work of teachers, we strive to provide materials and programs that are at once enlightening to the mind and ennobling to the heart; faithful and complete, as well as useful and practical.

Sophia Institute gratefully recognizes the Solidarity Association for preserving and encouraging the growth of our apostolate over the course of many years. Without their generous and timely support, this book would not be in your hands.

www.SophiaInstitute.com
www.CatholicExchange.com
www.SophiaTeachers.org

Sophia Institute Press is a registered trademark of Sophia Institute.
Sophia Institute is a tax-exempt institution as defined by the
Internal Revenue Code, Section 501(c)(3). Tax ID 22-2548708.